TROLLS

BY MELISSA GISH

CREATIVE EDUCATION • CREATIVE PAPERBACKS

MW00608953

Published by Creative Education and Creative Paperbacks
P.O. Box 227, Mankato, Minnesota 56002
Creative Education and Creative Paperbacks are imprints of
The Creative Company
www.thecreativecompany.us

Design by The Design Lab
Production by Rachel Klimpel
Art direction by Rita Marshall
Printed in the United States of America

Photographs by Alamy (Chronicle), Creative Commons Wikimedia
(John Bauer, Cyrille R. W. Chaussepied, Mårten Eskil Winge), Devi-
ant Art (bridge-troll, BrokenMachine86, eoghankerrigan, Minnha-
gen), Dreamstime (Stefan Holm), Flickr (Kjetil Øvrebø), Shutterstock
(Barandash Karandashich, Teo Tarras), Unsplash.com (Fermin
Rodriguez Penelas)

Library of Congress Cataloging-in-Publication Data
Names: Gish, Melissa, author.
Title: Trolls / Melissa Gish.
Series: Amazing mysteries.
Includes bibliographical references and index.
Summary: A basic exploration of the appearance, behaviors, and
origins of trolls, the gigantic creatures of Scandinavian legend
known for their appetites. Also included is a story from folklore
about a troll in disguise.

Identifiers:
ISBN 978-1-64026-491-5 (hardcover)
ISBN 978-1-68277-042-9 (pbk)
ISBN 978-1-64000-618-8 (eBook)
This title has been submitted for CIP processing under LCCN
2021937339.

First Edition HC 9 8 7 6 5 4 3 2 1
First Edition PBK 9 8 7 6 5 4 3 2 1

Table of Contents

Old stories from Norway described trolls that lived in mountains or caves.

Trolls are creatures that stand nearly twice as tall as humans. They first appeared in tales written 800 years ago in **Scandinavia**. Some trolls are smart and helpful. Others are scary. They might even eat people!

Scandinavia the name for the part of the world where Denmark, Norway, and Sweden are; Iceland and Finland are sometimes included

Some trolls are humanlike. They make swords. They hide treasure but may share with kind humans. These trolls live in the forest and know how to heal illnesses.

Trolls can do a lot of damage, no matter what type of weapon they have.

Other trolls may be green and slimy or hairy and stinky. In Norway, the shaggy jötunn (*YOO-tun*) gobbles up travelers. The smaller þurs (*THOORS*) makes anyone it sees answer a riddle. A wrong answer gets them eaten!

Forest and mountain trolls can uproot trees and sometimes cause storms.

Trolls have eyes the size of plates. This helps them to see in the dark. Huge noses give them a sharp sense of smell. Trolls cut off their broken arms or legs. Then they grow new ones. Trolls hate noise. Sunlight turns them to stone.

People in Norway told of trolls stirring their hot cereals with their long noses.

Trolls called *fodden skemaend* (FO-dun skee-MOND) mine for treasure in caves. They kidnap people and force them to work in the mines.

Cave trolls are usually smaller than humans and try to trick people.

Inuit children who
believed the scary stories
were more likely to stay
away from the water.

Inuit stories tell of the qallupilluit

(*kah-LOO-pee-loo-EET*). These green trolls live in underwater caves. They swim in the icy water. They look for children who go out alone.

Inuit relating to the native people of northern Canada and parts of Greenland and Alaska

Rune stones date from hundreds of years ago, and many were raised during the time of the Vikings.

One of Finland's Åland (*OH-lond*) Islands is home to a "lake troll." **Rune stones** on the lakeshore keep the troll underwater. But fog blocks the magic. People have to be careful when they take their boats out on a foggy day.

rune stones stones carved with signs or letters believed to have magical properties

In stories from northern Europe, Thor is the god of storms. He often throws lightning on trolls, killing them. Fire is still known as the best weapon against trolls.

Thor used his hammer, Mjölnir, to bring lightning down on his enemies.

In J. R. R. Tolkien's Middle-earth, the Olog-hai is a terrible troll that can withstand sunshine. In the world of Harry Potter, wild mountain trolls are destructive. Troll dolls have colorful hair. People like watching movies about them!

The evil ruler Sauron made the Olog-hai from a mix of mountain and cave trolls.

One day, a man came to a river. He stepped into the water to swim across. Just then, a gnarled, old log floated up. It bumped him. *How fortunate*, the man thought. He climbed on top of it and began to paddle through the water. Halfway across the river, the log laughed. The man screamed. This was no log. It was a troll in disguise. And it meant to eat him.

Read More

Lawrence, Sandra. *The Atlas of Monsters*. Philadelphia: Running Press Kids, 2019.

London, Martha. *Trolls*. Minneapolis: Pop!, 2020.

Peebles, Alice. *Giants and Trolls*. Minneapolis: Hungry Tomato, 2016.

Websites

Guide to Iceland: Folklore in Iceland
https://guidetoiceland.is/history-culture/folklore-in-iceland
Read about the history of trolls in Iceland.

Owlcation: Trolls of Norway—Facts and Fiction
https://owlcation.com/social-sciences/troll-of-norway
Find out what people in Norway think about trolls.

Note: Every effort has been made to ensure that the websites listed above are suitable for children, that they have educational value, and that they contain no inappropriate material. However, because of the nature of the Internet, it is impossible to guarantee that these sites will remain active indefinitely or that their contents will not be altered.

Index